**YOUR FAVORITE STARS**

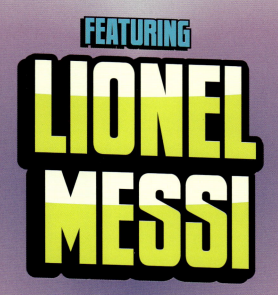

# FEATURING
# LIONEL MESSI

## FACTS, QUIZZES, ACTIVITIES, AND MORE!

by Matt Chandler

CAPSTONE PRESS
a capstone imprint

This is an unauthorized biography.

Published by Capstone Press, an imprint of Capstone
1710 Roe Crest Drive, North Mankato, Minnesota 56003
capstonepub.com

Copyright © 2026 by Capstone. All rights reserved. No part of this publication may be reproduced in whole or in part, or stored in a retrieval system, or transmitted in any form or by any means, electronic, mechanical, photocopying, recording, or otherwise, without written permission of the publisher.

Library of Congress Cataloging-in-Publication Data is available on the Library of Congress website.

ISBN: 9798875233012 (hardcover)
ISBN: 9798875232961 (paperback)
ISBN: 9798875232978 (ebook PDF)

Summary: A collection of fun facts, photos, and more, perfect for fans of soccer superstar Lionel Messi.

Editorial Credits
Editor: Julie Gassman; Designer: Elyse White; Media Researcher: Rebekah Hunstenberger; Production Specialist: Tori Abraham

Image Credits
Alamy: Joan Valls/Urbanandsport/NurPhoto SRL, 39, Cao Can/Xinhua, 25; Getty Images: Alexandre Schneider, 17 (top), David Ramos, 21 (top), Elsa, 4, Gilbert Carrasquillo/GC Images, 32, Joe Raedle, 6, Kevin C. Cox, 37, 41, Lars Baron, 9, Marcelo Boeri/El Grafico, 14, Matthias Hangst, 29, Megan Briggs, 40, 47, Pascal Le Segretain, 45, Phillip Faraone, 10 (middle left), Rick Kern, 10 (bottom right), Rodrigo Valle, 7, Ronald Martinez, 11 (Lionel Messi), Slaven Vlasic, 10 (top right), Tim Nwachukwu, front cover (Lionel Messi), 31 (Lionel Messi); Shutterstock: ANNA ZASIMOVA (rainbow chrome star), back cover and throughout, BARBARA LOPEZ, 5, Brovko Serhii (soccer ball), cover and throughout, 43 (net), derter (rainbow chrome sparkle), back cover and throughout, em_concepts (Argentina flag), front cover, 28, 46, Evgenia Vasileva, 38 (black heart), Fabideciria, 19, He2, 12, JosepPerianes, 30 (music notes), Lahya Creative, 27 (controller), lanastace, 35 (top right), Lauritta, cover (soccer trophy), LeonART Studio, 31 (headphones), lilia_ahapova, 36 (heart), Maciej Rogowski Photo, 42, MariaLev, 22 (Paris Saint Germain logo), 23 (Barcelona FC logo), Marynova, 33, Mashaart (silver chrome star), back cover and throughout, Mehadi Hasan Ridoy, 23 (Argentina National Team logo), NOMONARTS, 16, Rahmad900, 23 (player silhouette), Red Vector, 21 (cookie), shiji1 (sparkle), 13, 34, v_kulieva (blurry hearts background), back cover and throughout, vectspace, 22 (Intermiami logo), Wirestock Creators, 34, Yuliia Sobolieva (sparkle stars), 17, 38, 41, zainabsoly, 26 (key)

*Stats are current through February 2025.

Printed and bound in China. 6274

# TABLE OF CONTENTS

**CHAPTER 1:**
**MESSI MAGIC** ........................4

**CHAPTER 2:**
**MAKING OF A SUPERSTAR** ....12

**CHAPTER 3:**
**DOMINATING THE PITCH** .......18

**CHAPTER 4:**
**OFF FIELD** ...........................26

**CHAPTER 5:**
**GIVING BACK** ......................34

**CHAPTER 6:**
**WHAT'S NEXT?** ...................40

CHAPTER **1**

# MESSI MAGIC

## SOCIAL SUPERSTAR

Messi's popularity on the pitch has made him one of the biggest sports stars on social media. Check out how many followers he has!

**YOUTUBE:**
**3.97 MILLION**

**FACEBOOK:**
**117 MILLION**

**X (ADIDAS-SPONSORED PAGE): 3.5 MILLION**

**INSTAGRAM:**
**504 MILLION**

**LIONEL MESSI** has millions of fans around the globe! When he joined **Inter Miami** in 2023, more than 20,000 fans braved a rainstorm to welcome him. His introduction drew more than 3.5 BILLION views online. His Inter Miami jersey (Number 10) was the best-selling jersey in Major League Soccer (MLS) in 2024. But it's the stats and accomplishments he's had on the pitch that have made Messi a soccer legend.

# EXPERIENCE MESSI

When Messi signed with Inter Miami, he instantly became the biggest soccer star to ever join MLS. Fans packed the stadium in July 2023, not to watch a match, but just to welcome Messi to Miami! His popularity was so huge, a 20,000-square-foot building was designed to house "**The Messi Experience: A Dream Come True**." More than 50,000 fans visited The Messi Experience in the first two months it was open.

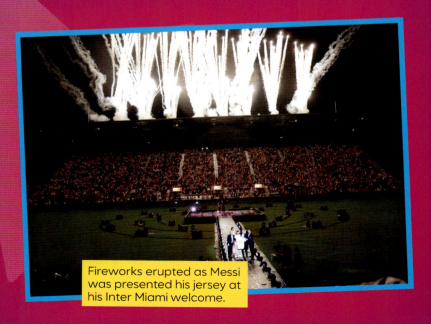

Fireworks erupted as Messi was presented his jersey at his Inter Miami welcome.

# WHAT FANS CAN DO INSIDE THE MESSI EXPERIENCE

1. Learn what it was like to be part of a World Cup win from inside Argentina's locker room.

2. Practice hands-on soccer skills.

3. Take selfies "with" the soccer superstar thanks to amazing technology.

## STAR SCOOP!

Countless fans idolize Messi so much they get the superstar's face and name tattooed on their bodies!

# WORD PLAY

Fill in the blank with a word from the list to learn some fun facts about Lionel Messi.

1. _____ is Messi's favorite television show.

2. Messi loves sweets. One of his favorite sweet treats is _____.

3. _____ was the soccer star Messi idolized when he was growing up.

4. Messi leases a _____ that is estimated to be worth $15 million.

5. Crypto company _____ pays Messi $20 million per year to be their spokesperson.

**6.** Do you have any pets? Messi does. Abu is his _____.

**7.** Of all the superstars he has played with, _____ is one of Messi's all-time favorites.

- PABLO AIMAR
- TOY POODLE
- NEYMAR JR.
- PRIVATE JET
- DULCE DE LECHE
- SOCIOS
- *GAME OF THRONES*

Answers: 1. *Game of Thrones*, 2. Dulce de leche, 3. Pablo Aimar, 4. Private jet, 5. Socios, 6. Toy poodle, 7. Neymar Jr.

# LOVED BY HIS PEERS

Messi is incredibly popular among his fellow athletes. Here's what a few had to say:

"Seeing Messi, the GOAT of soccer, honor the MLS with his presence is a total game-changer for us."
**—Basketball superstar LeBron James**

 "I love Messi, he is a great player."
**—Super Bowl champion Tom Brady**

"There is no one else in the game that compares to Messi. He just is so fun to watch."
**—Olympic gold medalist Alex Morgan**

## STAR SCOOP!

Messi learned about one of his fans, 100-year-old Don Hernan. The superfan kept a notebook in which he records all of Messi's goals scored. The superstar made a personalized video and sent it to Hernan to show his appreciation!

## CHAPTER 2
# MAKING OF A SUPERSTAR

As early as anyone can remember, Messi could be found dribbling a soccer ball. If he didn't have a ball, that didn't stop him. He would make a ball out of plastic bags, kicking it down the streets of his neighborhood. By the time he was 11, his family knew he had a future in soccer. "He had a very personal sense of motivation," his dad, Jorge, said. "He always loved soccer."

### STAR SCOOP!

When Messi was 13, his family left Argentina and moved to Spain. Messi joined Barcelona, and his life as a professional soccer player began!

# MAKE A SOCCER BALL!

## WHAT YOU NEED:

- 20-30 plastic grocery bags
- 1-2 sheets of newspaper
- String or twine

## WHAT YOU DO:

1. Scrunch up the newspaper into a ball. Place the newspaper ball in a grocery bag. Twist the bag around the ball.

2. Hold the ball and pull the rest of the bag over it, twisting it again. Repeat until you run out of bag. Tie off the bag with a knot at the handles. Repeat with more bags, until the ball is the size you want it.

3. Wrap the string around the ball a few times. Turn the ball 90 degrees and wrap the string around the ball some more. Turn another 45 degrees and wrap again. Continue with as much string as you like, weaving it in and out for added strength.

4. When you are happy with the ball, tie off the string, and give your ball a dribble!

# YOUNG LEO

Messi shares some thoughts on growing up in Argentina:

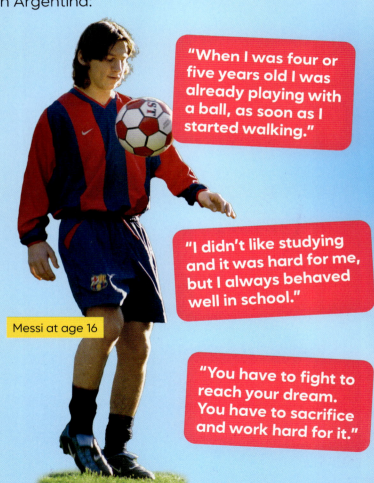

"When I was four or five years old I was already playing with a ball, as soon as I started walking."

Messi at age 16

"I didn't like studying and it was hard for me, but I always behaved well in school."

"You have to fight to reach your dream. You have to sacrifice and work hard for it."

# TRACKING HIS TEAMS

| YEARS | TEAM | COUNTRY |
|---|---|---|
| 1992–1995 | Grandoli | Argentina |
| 1995–2000 | Newell's Old Boys | Argentina |
| 2000–2021 | Barcelona FC | Spain |
| 2021–2023 | Paris St. Germain | France |
| 2023– | Inter Miami | United States |

## STAR SCOOP!

Messi's first contract to play pro soccer was written and signed on the back of a paper napkin. In 2024, that napkin was sold at auction for **$965,000**!

# A ROUGH START

Five years after he joined Barcelona, Messi earned the call up to Argentina's national club. On August 17, 2005, the teenager came off the bench in a friendly against Hungary.

Less than one minute into Messi's time on the pitch, Hungarian defender **VILMOS VANCZAK** grabbed the back of Messi's jersey to slow down the speedy youngster. Messi swung back and his elbow struck Vanczak. Vanczak went down hard. Messi received a **RED CARD** and was sent off. His debut was a disaster. Fortunately for Argentina, he would bounce back to become the all-time leading scorer in his country's history.

## STAR SCOOP!

Despite his rough start, Messi learned his lesson. Twenty years after his debut, he has received only two more red cards.

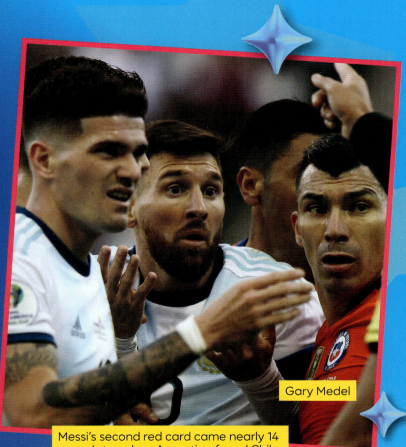

Gary Medel

Messi's second red card came nearly 14 years later when Argentina faced Chile in the 2019 Copa America. Messi argued with Chilean defender Gary Medel, and a ref sent them both off the field.

# CHAPTER 3
# DOMINATING THE PITCH

For all his awards and records, none may be more impressive than the **2022 World Cup**. Messi had the chance to bring the cup home to Argentina in 2014, but his team fell short. But in 2022, he delivered.

Messi dominated the tournament as he led Argentina to a Finals face-off against France. With the Cup on the line, Messi took over. He scored two of his team's three goals in regulation. He added a crucial goal on a penalty kick. Argentina captured the World Cup!

### STAR SCOOP!

Messi is the only player in history to score in every match of a World Cup Knockout Round!

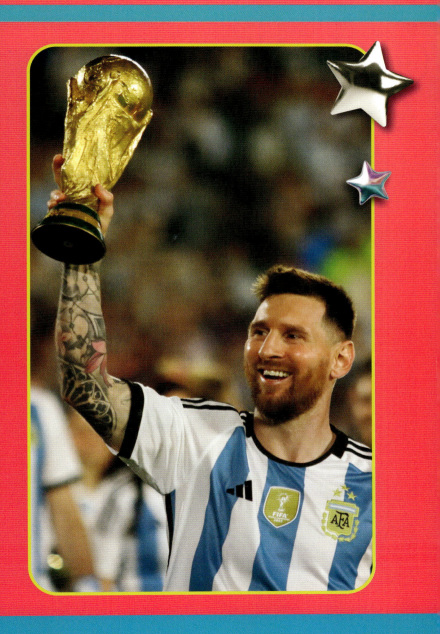

# quiz!

## SCORING MACHINE
What do you know about the GOAT's goals?

**1.** Messi scored a career-high 50 goals in a single season. What team did he play for?

**2.** Only two players have scored more than 800 career goals. Messi is one. Who is the other?

**3.** Messi's goal scoring earned him a spot in Guinness World Records. Can you guess what goal-scoring record he set?

**4.** As of February 2025, Messi has accomplished what major scoring "trick" 59 times in his incredible career?

## STAR SCOOP!

When Messi was a boy, one coach motivated him by giving him a cookie every time he scored a goal. If he scored on a header, he received two cookies!

1. Messi tallied 50 goals as a member of Barcelona in 2011/12. 2. Cristiano Ronaldo has scored more than 900 goals in his career! 3. Messi was recognized for scoring 91 total goals in 2012. 4. A hat trick—three goals in a single game.

# GOAL!

Messi is considered one of the greatest goal scorers in history. By the end of his second season with Inter Miami, Messi had scored 850 career goals—second most all-time to his rival Ronaldo. Check out his tally by team:

**BARCELONA: 672 GOALS**

**ARGENTINA (NATIONAL TEAM): 112 GOALS**

**PARIS SAINT-GERMAIN: 32 GOALS**

**INTER MIAMI: 36 GOALS**

### STAR SCOOP!

Messi's 474 goals in LaLiga action for Barcelona set the record for most goals in LaLiga league history.

## DRAW MESSI'S KIT!

Want to show off your drawing skills? Use this outline to trace Messi onto a piece of drawing paper. Then draw him in your favorite uniform from his amazing career. Which uniform will your Messi be wearing? His first team, Barcelona? His national team, Argentina? Paris Saint-Germain, where he scored his 700th goal? Or his most recent team, Inter Miami?

# RACKING UP AWARDS

Messi is one of the most decorated soccer players of all time! Here are just *some* of the awards he has captured in his incredible career:

## INDIVIDUAL HONORS

**8 BALLOONS D'OR:** 2009, 2010, 2011, 2012, 2015, 2019, 2021, 2023

**6 EUROPEAN GOLDEN BOOTS:** 2009/10, 2011/12, 2012/13, 2016/17, 2017/18, 2018/19

**9 LALIGA MOST VALUABLE PLAYERS:** 2008/09, 2009/10, 2010/11, 2011/12, 2012/13, 2014/15, 2016/17, 2017/18, 2018/19

**2 WORLD CUP GOLDEN BALLS:** 2014, 2022

**2 COPA AMÉRICA MOST VALUABLE PLAYERS:** 2015, 2021

# TEAM CHAMPIONSHIPS

**FIFA WORLD CUP:** 2022

**FINALISSIMA:** 2022

**COPA AMÉRICA:** 2021

**OLYMPIC GOLD MEDAL:** 2008

**U-20 WORLD CUP:** 2005

## STAR SCOOP!

In 2009, Messi was named the FIFA World Player of the Year. He collected 1,073 points in the voting, 721 points more than second-place finisher Cristiano Ronaldo.

CHAPTER **4**

# OFF FIELD

## MORE THAN A SOCCER SUPERSTAR!

quiz!

How much do you know about Messi off the pitch? Take this quiz and test your fandom:

**1.** Messi signed an endorsement deal with a shoe company that pays him $21 million per year. What shoes does he wear?

    A. Adidas
    B. Nike
    C. Puma

**2.** How many homes does Messi own?

    A. One
    B. Four
    C. Eleven

Messi loves sporty cars. In 2016 he outbid another soccer star to buy a rare 1957 Ferrari 335 S Spider Scaglietti. Which superstar did he outbid to get his new wheels?

A. David Beckham
B. Cristiano Ronaldo
C. Neymar Jr.

 Which team does Messi choose when he is playing FIFA on his PlayStation?

A. Argentina's National Team
B. Chelsea
C. Manchester United

 When he was a child, Messi's older brothers gave him a nickname that stuck with him to this day. What did they call him?

A. La Pulga (The Flea)
B. El Pollo (The Chicken)
C. La Plaga (The Pest)

Answers: 1. A, 2. B, 3. B, 4. B, 5. A

# THE KING OF FASHION

Off the pitch, Messi loves to look fashionable. He arrived at the 2022 World Cup wearing a white gold watch worth more than $145,000! He attends events dressed in custom Armani suits. He even designed two popular pairs of Adidas sneakers!

His love of fashion led Messi to launch his own clothing line, **Messi Brand**. "I like to explore different fields that are of interest besides sport," he said. "I always try to make the most of every opportunity to be a part of something new and exciting."

## STAR SCOOP!

In 2022 Messi led Argentina to the World Cup. The next year, one out of every 70 babies (1.4 percent) born in Argentina was named **LIONEL** or **LIONELA**.

# PREGAME PLAYLIST

Many players listen to music to get pumped before a game. Messi said, "Music calms my mind, helping me maintain composure and relaxation." He has his own warm-up playlist. Some of the superstar's pregame jams include:

**RIHANNA: "DON'T STOP THE MUSIC"**

**PITBULL: "I KNOW YOU WANT ME"**

**BAD BUNNY: "MONACO"**

**CELIA CRUZ: "LA VIDA ES UN CARNAVAL"**

**SERGIO TORRES: "MIRA COMO BAILA"**

# THE NAME OF FAME

Imagine being so famous people name things after you. Messi doesn't have to imagine, that dream is real. He can visit his home country of Argentina and drive down **Lionel Messi Avenue**. If he gets hungry, the soccer star can stop at a Hard Rock Cafe and order a **Messi Chicken Sandwich**. Even the Argentinian national soccer team's training facility feels familiar. In 2023, it was renamed "**Lionel Andres Messi**"!

# 5 OF LIONEL MESSI'S BIGGEST PURCHASES:

1. **1957 FERRARI 335 S SPIDER SCAGLIETTI:** $36 MILLION
2. **LUXURY SPANISH HOTEL:** $30.5 MILLION
3. **GULFSTREAM V PRIVATE JET:** $15 MILLION
4. **CONDOMINIUM IN SUNNY ISLES BEACH, FLORIDA:** $7.3 MILLION
5. **MANSION IN BARCELONA, SPAIN:** $7 MILLION

## STAR SCOOP!

By the end of 2024, Messi had earned roughly $1.6 billion in his career and scored 850 goals. That breaks down to more than $1.8 million for EVERY goal he has scored.

CHAPTER **5**

# GIVING BACK

Sports superstars are role models to millions of fans. Messi has used his fame to make a difference around the world. In 2007 he launched the **Leo Messi Foundation**. Messi focuses on helping children at risk in many different situations. He partners with hospitals and other groups to support children in need.

Children play soccer in Rosario, Argentina. The Leo Messi Foundation has supported many projects for children in Rosario, Messi's hometown.

# 5 FOUNDATION PROJECTS:

Paid for 20 classrooms to be built in Syria for 1,600 students to attend school

Donated $1.1 million to Clinic Barcelona in Argentina to fight the COVID-19 pandemic

Gave more than $300,000 to UNICEF to support humanitarian aid for children

Donated $218,000 to provide access to free food and clean water for 2,000 Kenyans

Provided more than $2.7 million in funding for Barcelona's SJD Pediatric Cancer Center

## STAR SCOOP!

In 2019, *Forbes* named Messi the highest-paid athlete in the world. He earned more than $127 million that year. He is generous with his fortune.

# OVERCOMING LONG ODDS

When he was 11 years old, Messi was diagnosed with a rare disorder known as **Growth Hormone Deficiency** (GHD). GHD slowed down his growth, and Messi was always the smallest boy at school and on the pitch. To treat his disease, Messi had to have medicine injected in his leg every night for years.

When he was 14, Messi no longer needed the injections. The help and care he received during his childhood is one of the reasons he is so dedicated to charitable causes that benefit children.

## STAR SCOOP!

During the COVID-19 pandemic, Messi donated more than one million euros to aid in healthcare in his home country of Argentina.

# WISHES COME TRUE

Zack Morehouse is a young soccer player from Wisconsin who battles Becker muscular dystrophy. The disease attacks the muscles in his body, weakening them. Messi has been one of Zack's biggest inspirations as he deals with the effects of the disease.

In 2024, the Make-A-Wish Foundation coordinated a chance for Zack to meet his idol. Messi brought Zack and his family to Florida. He got to talk with Messi and pose for photos. Zack is one of dozens of children Messi has supported through Make-A-Wish.

Messi poses with children who were treated at Hospital Sant Joan de Déu.

## STAR SCOOP!

While a member of Barcelona, Messi donated more than three million euros to create a cancer unit focusing on the care of young children at Barcelona's Hospital Sant Joan de Déu in Spain.

## CHAPTER 6
# WHAT'S NEXT?

If Inter Miami turns out to be Messi's last club, he is going out on top. In his first game with Inter Miami on July 21, 2023, Messi delivered. He entered the match as a substitute in the 54th minute. With the game tied at 1, Messi took a hard hit and was awarded a free kick. With 20,512 fans cheering him on, he curled a perfect kick over the outstretched arms of Cruz Azul goalkeeper Andrés Gudiño for the game-winning goal!

Messi and Inter Miami went on to win the **2023 Leagues Cup**. It was the 44th title of Messi's career!

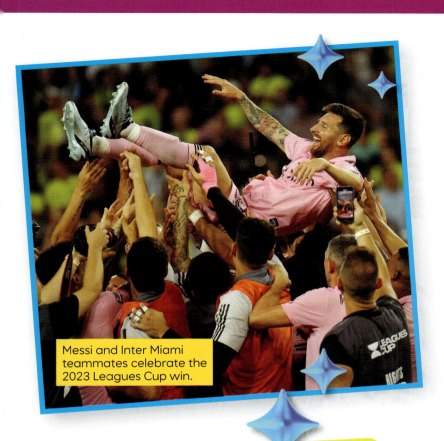

Messi and Inter Miami teammates celebrate the 2023 Leagues Cup win.

## STAR SCOOP!

Messi has talked about one day sharing his knowledge of the game by becoming a sporting director.

# MIAMI MAGIC

Only one player has scored more goals than Messi: **Cristiano Ronaldo**. Messi may not catch Ronaldo for the all-time goals record, but he is sure trying. On October 19, 2024, the 36-year-old Messi tallied a hat trick for Inter Miami to crush the New England Revolution 6–2. He finished the season tied for second in MLS with 20 goals. He led the league with 36 combined goals and assists for the season!

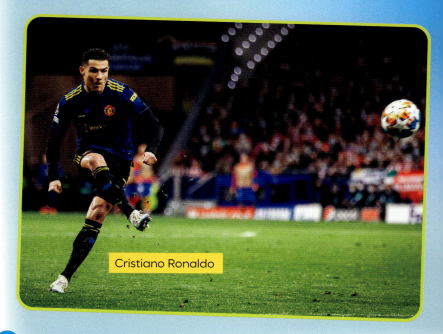

Cristiano Ronaldo

# ALL-TIME TOP GOAL SCORERS

- **CRISTIANO RONALDO:** 925 GOALS
- **LIONEL MESSI:** 852 GOALS
- **JOSEF BICAN:** 805 GOALS
- **ROMÁRIO:** 772 GOALS
- **PELÉ:** 757 GOALS
- **FERENC PUSKÁS:** 746 GOALS
- **GERD MÜLLER:** 734 GOALS
- **FERENC DEÁK:** 576 GOALS
- **UWE SEELER:** 575 GOALS
- **TÚLIO MARAVILHA:** 575 GOALS

# SMASHING RECORDS ON THE PITCH

Messi holds dozens of records. Here are some of his biggest:

**MOST BALLON D'OR AWARDS:** 8

**MOST ESM GOLDEN BOOT AWARDS:** 6

**ALL-TIME GOALS LEADER FOR LALIGA:** 474

**MOST INDIVIDUAL WORLD CUP APPEARANCES:** 26

**ALL-TIME GOALS LEADER FOR ARGENTINA:** 112

**MOST ASSISTS, ALL-TIME:** 381